STAGE-CRAFT

for
CHRISTMAS and EASTER PLAYS

A method of simplified staging
for the church

JAMES HULL MILLER

MERIWETHER PUBLISHING LTD.
Colorado Springs, Colorado

Meriwether Publishing Ltd., Publisher
P.O. Box 7710
Colorado Springs, CO 80933

Editor: Arthur Zapel and Ted Zapel
Typesetting: Sharon Garlock
Cover design: K. Anne Kircher

Library of Congress Cataloging-in-Publication Data

Miller, James Hull.
    Stagecraft for Christmas and Easter plays : a method of simplified staging for the church / by James Hull Miller.
       p.   cm.
   ISBN 0-916260-64-X
    1. Theaters--Stage-setting and scenery. 2. Christian drama--Presentation, etc. 3. Drama in Christian education.   I. Title.
PN2091.S8M49564   1990
792'.025--dc20
                                   89-49383
                                      CIP

STAGE-CRAFT

for
CHRISTMAS and EASTER
PLAYS

TABLE OF CONTENTS

INTRODUCTION

The editors of Meriwether Publishing Ltd. asked me to write a scenic book as a companion piece to their very popular **Costuming the Christmas and Easter Play**.

Now it is one thing to costume an actor for a certain part and quite another to build sets for the same play. Once costumed for that certain part an actor can move through many different staging spaces. However, this does not remain true for sets. For a set must not only relate to a certain play, but it must also relate to the shape of the playing space and the ambience of its decor. Thus, for each costume in stock in the wardrobe chest, many, many sets may be required.

When the player is in a church, the church is all around him — whether it be the stone walls of a Gothic cathedral, the white walls and shuttered windows of a New England meeting room or an open platform at the end of a contemporary sanctuary. Obviously any scenery in these finished spaces will appear in much the same way that "props" appear in the finished space of a store window; that is, neither the set in the church nor the props in the store window are directly related to the spaces they are in, but can be likened to units of sculpture in an art gallery.

By contrast, the "picture frame" stage of a proscenium theatre contains a vacancy that is meant to be filled with scenery of a highly "pictorial" nature in the same way that a motion picture screen or television tube is filled up with literal imagery.

We are so accustomed to the "picture" tradition that we take it for granted; yet when we look at merchandise through a store window, the display person may have managed to suggest not only the season, but also the geographical location, all by means of just a few scattered props or set pieces.

1

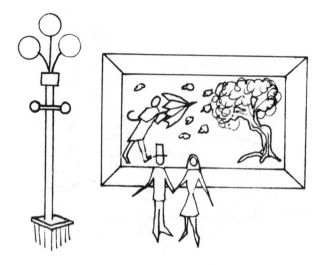

In reality, we are not looking for a "picture" at all: we are seeking *information* — the imagination supplies the rest. Even in the proscenium theatre the audience is fully aware that the fabulous one-point perspective of an opera backdrop does not really extend beyond the picture frame; that if one went backstage he would find himself in that wickedly seductive area our Victorian forebears referred to as "behind the scenes" (not to mention disembodied pieces of scenery scattered about like wreckage from some "Twilight Zone"). Yet the illusion holds nonetheless, a tribute to a human psychological bent known as "the persistence of vision."

Around 1300, Giotto began painting pictures into which the viewers felt they were walking, a style which found expression in the theatre from Renaissance times by means of a proscenium frame. This is the "snapshot" view, one which places heavy emphasis on the particular place from which a scene is viewed. Still, it is not always thus. Take, for example, Oriental scroll painting: a scene seems to unwind upwards, with mountains stacked one upon another. Where is the spectator here? Look closely — you may find him in the form of a tiny figure in a boat or on a rock with a fishing pole in his hand. The "picture" here is the *consciousness* of where he is and what he may be comtemplating. We, the overall viewers, *are informed* and an illusion follows.

A different example is a medieval tapestry scene depicting a pilgrimage through many fields, woods and villages by means of miniaturization by which the scope of an entire journey is revealed.

In these two examples we have *conceptual* perspective, not *visual* perspective. In many early religious paintings the actual size of people often has more to do with their thematic importance than with their actual positions in space.

Let us now enter the world of the church and see what confronts a designer of a biblical play! As the book unfolds the reader will become acutely aware that there are no ready-made solutions for specific scenes,

2

that design decisions end up taking into account the talent pool, short-versus long-term use, and available time and materials, not to mention old "tried-and-true" chestnuts (such as a triptych of curtained Gothic arches I built from a Yamaha piano crate and which I have used on and off ever since).

Chapter 1:

Some Design Principles of Space Staging

I am a designer by profession, a "scene technician," with a wide variety of backstage experience ranging from summer theatres and jitney touring companies to formal academic production and architectural consulting. However, my initiation to staging in the church came about in a strictly *pro bono* way.

My wife and I and our three children attended services in a small Presbyterian church. At the approach of the Christmas season the men of the church began preparations for a biblical play by covering the walls of the sanctuary adjacent to the pulpit with large sheets of paper on which scenes of Jerusalem had been painted. This attempt to conceal the white woodwork and shutters with a pictorial background I considered futile.

I said nothing at the time; however, the following year I suggested a different approach, that of placing something dramatic at the heart of the altar space instead of around it.

The rough sketch gives the gist of my proposal. The tower, borrowed from our children's theatre repertory, represented the inn. The stables were suggested by some arches and a roof piece. The elevated platform

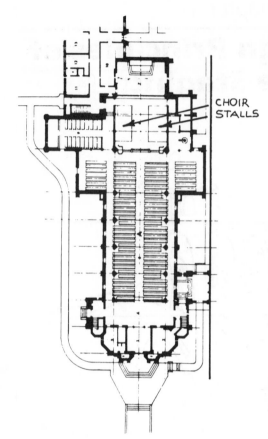

CHOIR
STALLS

straddled a dais with an immovable altar rail, the pulpit and lectern having been removed. The center steps led to an aisle, the flanking steps to side aisles.

The sketch on page 5 illustrates many of the cardinal points of space stage design: visibility, profile, a central imagery, strong architectural form and adequate paths for stage movement.

The platform was the usual three-quarter inch plyboard nailed to ribs for clamping or bolting. Sawhorses (of which two are shown) were custom built to accommodate the change of level from the church floor to the dais with its altar rail.

In any design it is extremely important that the storage of parts and ease of assembly be considered from the beginning, for not only do rehearsals have a way of exceeding the free time between services but weddings and funerals have a way of popping up unexpectedly.

Not too long after my successful entry into church theatricals and seasonal pageants, my daughters (loyal choir members for many years) were lured away by a rival choirmaster and I found myself nodding in the dim stone recesses of a marvelous Gothic edifice, with processional footfalls clacking over great slabs of blue gray slate. Awed by these bushels of grandeur I hid my light and waited to see what the Christmas season would bring.

Led by a local television executive, the men of the church again attempted to "bury" the architecture, this time not with paper murals but with proscenium-style "flats" whose successful erection was made possible only by covering the slate floor with heavy plywood panels into which conventional stage braces were anchored.

By the following season, however, my former church activities had become known and the choirmaster approached me for assistance. I of course demurred, saying the sort of solution that I had recently witnessed was definitely not up my alley.

"But that's precisely why I'm asking *you*," he quickly replied. "I know it's all wrong, too."

And so began nearly twenty years on slate and marble with even more immovable features to surmount, but with an overall surround considerably richer than New England church architecture. And in addition to my own custom-built scenery I managed to use most of the sets I had built for a number of touring groups, both sacred and profane, my reputation for freestanding scenery having grown apace. I was now known as the man who needed only a flat floor of any material on which to place my scenery.

Unfortunately in this particular church there was not a great deal of unobstructed floor area and the presence of opposing choir stalls in the chancel left some eleven feet of free space.

My first production was Benjamin Britten's *Noye's Fludde,* with a medieval style suggested. For purposes of our discussion, the concept drawing below is all that is necessary .

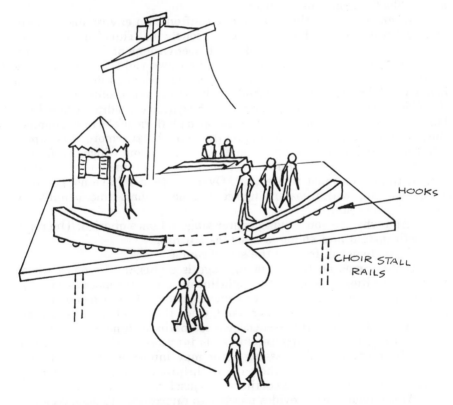

The ark's deck consisted of a 6' x 16' platform (two 4x8s and two 2x8s bolted together) set both on sawhorses and on the forward choir stall rails. A ramp led from the center aisle of the nave and steps descended into the chancel near the altar rail.

As the play began, a large tree, simulated by a long rug roll with a disk of foliage, was cut down to become the mast. The ark's gunwales were in three sections, with the center section clamped in place after the animals had passed by. Since the choir stall rails were 4'-9" high the animals descending the steps to the rear disappeared from view — presumably into the bowels of the ship; the principals remained on deck for the singing. With the last gunwale in place, a large blue cloth of a shimmering material was hooked to the gunwales by dark-clad "serviteurs de la scène," thus covering the ramp and the marble bases flanking the steps from the nave to the chancel.

With such a platform thrust up into the ambience of the church architecture, its structural masking was important. So I spent a small fortune on a deep brown velveteen fabric "Velcroed" to the sides of the platform and ramp. This material gave the appeearearance of "melting" into the dark-stained woodwork and gray stones around it, causing the ark to "float" in the church space.

When staging in the church, one confronts an environment where architectural integrity has already been concluded. Thus it is important that any visual elements added to this environment are essentially sculptural in nature and are objects in their own right. These elements should have both satisfactory texture and significant profile; texture to blend with the architectural "feel" of the space and profile to separate the added elements. Whether one is dealing with a cathedral, a New England town meeting room interior, or the open platform of the televangelist, the principles of space staging remain the same. Furthermore, it is important that a setting become a focal point of interest about which the dramatic action swirls. The set must never become a "container" of the action; rather, the action must relate to it. Over the years I have noticed that actors, working with freestanding scenery for the first time, usually try to crowd center stage.

"And why are you moving center stage?" I once queried. The reply was both instant and, to me at least, astonishing.

"Why, to get in front of the set, of course."

Diagrammed on the following page is a cluster of *profiles* whose lower extremities pass below the sightline over a platform and step unit. These profiles need only be offset by inches, but if they touch one another believability is lost. On the other hand, when they are too far separated, the illusion of space is threatened by a too realistic dimensionality.

In turn, if the aggregate cluster is too close to the platform and steps, the proximity of a passing actor may interfere with the profile statement. I suggest having the parts of the profile cluster three-quarter inch apart and the closest part of the profile just beyond an actor's reach.

Archway unit #6 provides us with an interesting illusion. Note the pure open profile against the distant trees, with the complete archway indicated, probably through some shading up to the dashed line. The remaining embrasures can either be open, or closed by fabrics which can then be made to glow by backlighting.

8

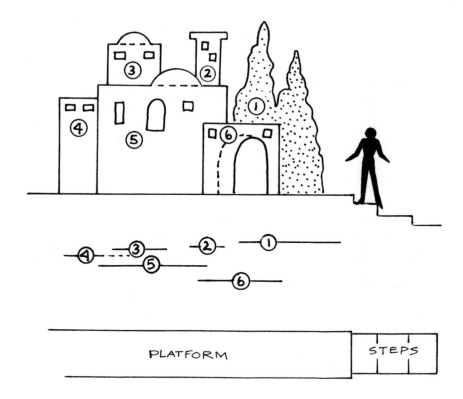

It is unnecessary — even undesirable — to attempt a visual relationship between the actor and the profiled background. Remember we are giving information, not illusion.

I realize that it may be difficult for those saturated with movies and television to believe that this particular example could be convincing. I myself would have doubted it had I not seen drawings made by children who had seen productions employing freestanding scenes in informal spaces. Much to my amazement, such scenery was usually redrawn to fit the *shape* of the paper, 8½" x 11", similar to a proscenium picture frame. On the other hand, give these same children some corrugated cardboard sheets, a utility knife, glue and tape and they will come up with a true space stage set.

An abstract style permits symbols to represent objects that are very large in real life. Study the profiles of buildings, then reduce these profiles to a convenient size for the space at hand.

A ramped playing surface is a very useful sort of platforming and I am listing six reasons which recommend it.

1. Since a ramped playing surface usually begins on the floor (for stage movement if for nothing else) its stability is derived in large part from the floor contact.

2. A ramped surface makes a very powerful statement! It throws any person or any thing placed upon it into sharp relief (profile again). In many cases the ramp *becomes* the background, since the eye is drawn to it.

3. It enhances visibility just like the old sloped stages of the nineteenth century which were coupled to flat floor seating for a wider range of activities.

4. Acoustics are improved. Choral risers accomplish the same thing, though they are good for little else.

5. In some ways a ramped structure is simpler to construct than an equivalent distance in risers and platforms. See Chapter 3.

6. A ramped platform easily passes over those flights of steps leading from the nave to the chancel, thus unifying these spaces in a very positive way.

Another effective device by which space staging can be organized is the pavilion or, in contemporary idiom, a gazebo. The pavilion draws its structural identity from the arch. For a source of ideas, study illustrations from medieval manuscripts and religious paintings of that era. Notice how many biblical scenes are "staged" by unrolling arches from church architecture.

The sketch below (left) is taken from a fourteenth century painting.

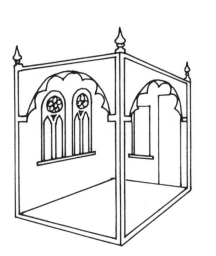

With these principles firmly in mind, let us look at a few typical scenes and see how they are solved in terms of what we have learned. I say "a few" because my aim is not a compendium of stock solutions but a system whereby, in a practical and original manner, the dramatists of the church can deal with any scene which may turn up, and this strictly in terms of the particular venue, the talent pool and available materials.

Then, after these typical scenes, the remaining chapters will deal with crafting, painting, lighting and "propping" them.

Chapter 2:

Typical Biblical Scenes

Early domestic architecture contains numerous examples of combinations of houses and barns. Detached barns and houses were exceptions, not the rule. The tower is a useful motif in freestanding scenery because it can be viewed from many angles. Just by attaching the stable to the tower its structure is considerably simplified.

The setting, (as illustrated on page 14) suitable for the Easter tomb scene, suggests a hillside with a grove of trees. The hillside profile conceals step units, which, by themselves, will be useful in many other situations. A rock slab provides an adjacent sitting space.

A profile tree (also on page 14) on a low platform plus an apron cloth of teasled velour suggests a lush hillside meadow for the Garden of Eden and numerous other nature settings. A perforated leaf pattern with taped-over color filters adds an interesting touch through skillful directional backlight. Color filter scraps can be changed seasonally.

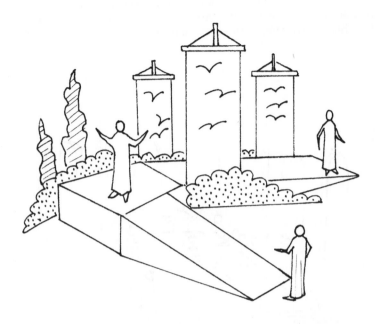

A double ramp maneuvers saintly figures into position for a heavenly scene. Profile cloud ground rows mask poles with gold banners of appliqued birds.

Due to the restrictive nature of a "box" setting with its containing three walls, interior or interior-related scenes are best handled by doorway groupings, using strongly silhouetted building shapes, plus the appropriate tables and benches. Fortunately, a set such as this is the most easily built of any of my scenery. Please refer to *Slabs* in Chapter 3.

The Last Supper and other banquet scenes can be quickly set up using side arch slabs flexibly hinge-clamped to a single arched frame. The flexible hinging permits a high degree of positioning in tight quarters.

Many scenes take place in public gathering places such as by gates and doorways to important buildings. In the sketch below a ramped platform leads to a public entrance into a fortified area.

In the sketch (top of page 17) a loggia is suggested, perhaps the site of the confrontation of Pilate and Christ. Here, levels assist with the degrees of authority. Since the architrave and columns are only indications of a larger environment a fabric canopy smoothes the transition into the reality of the church.

Prison scenes are all too familiar in the Bible. Here Sonotubes provide a space cutoff, while the arc of the backing piece plus the high set barred windows suggest confinement. See the painting chapter for notes on detailing the large stones.

Sonotubes are heavy cardboard cylinders for the containment of concrete in pouring piers. They are available at most construction supply centers. The spiral joints can be hidden by gluing on burlap.

This setting is taken from *Amahl and the Night Visitors*. A serpentine wall provides containment for the interior, yet the reverse curve relieves an otherwise sharp delineation between interior and exterior scenes. The platform and ramps at right provide a reasonable pattern of movement for travelers and shepherds approaching the shelter. Serpentine walls as sections of cylinders are described in Chapter 3.

This scene, taken from a fifteenth century painting, symbolizes the emergence of the new faith (greenery, vines, etc.) seen against the decay of traditional forms (decayed stonework of a classical age).

Technically, the rocks are made by profiling sheets of panel board and assembling them into wide slabs (see *Slab* construction, Chapter 3). Open sleeves of muslin are then glued down to form the thickness of the rocks. Art books provide a treasure trove of ideas for such set pieces.

INTRODUCTION TO THE
STAGECRAFT SECTION

"Keep it simple," the editors told me. "We know your other books provide the information needed, but the drama groups of smaller-sized churches are less experienced than full-time theatre people and would prefer more detailed information."

However, when I started writing, I soon realized that the book just wasn't going to work out exactly as planned. As I wrote at the beginning: "How can I design sets for dozens of different churches, each with their own plans and layouts plus their varying budgets and workers' skills? Would not such a book go on forever?"

But I did realize that this challenge had to be met head on one way or another.

So I laid out the foregoing as a "method of staging in the church" — any church — by sticking to concepts, concepts which do not change from church to church.

Then I plunged into the stagecraft itself, highlighting those techniques which I consider essential while bypassing others not absolutely necessary. A good example of this is found in the Lighting Section where I decided to "milk" 20-amp wall outlets and add to the illumination of the existing church lighting system instead of bringing in a lot of equipment and starting from scratch.

I also assumed that, of the dramatists of the church, some will be more advanced in basic craftsmanship than the beginners to which my other books are addressed.

So here we go into the Stagecraft section!

Chapter 3:

Building Scenery with Simple Tools

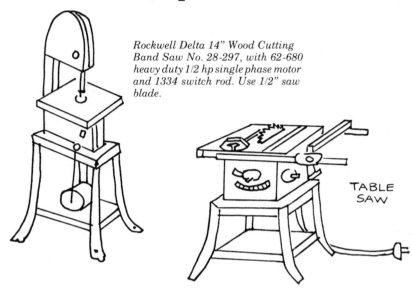

Rockwell Delta 14" Wood Cutting Band Saw No. 28-297, with 62-680 heavy duty 1/2 hp single phase motor and 1334 switch rod. Use 1/2" saw blade.

TABLE SAW

Rockwell Delta 9" Circular Tilting Arbor Bench Saw. Catalog No. 50-810 includes rip fence, guide bars, extension wings, miter gauge, blade.

Although it is my intention to keep tooling as simple as possible, it will be difficult to accomplish all the construction without a good table saw and a band saw. Since a lot of ripping will be necessary, a pull-over saw is not too useful — though if one is handy it can be used for cut-off work. Actually, one might assume that a group as diverse as one of a church membership will include someone with access to a manual arts shop in a school, but if not, the saws should be a cut above the grades found in the bargain bins of home builder's supply centers. The band saw should be of the two wheel type and the table saw need be no larger than one with an eight-inch or nine-inch blade. Sears products are okay; Delta is better.

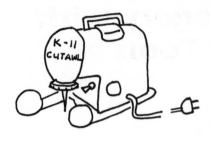

There is one other very useful tool that you will probably have to purchase unless you know someone in the display trade. This is a Cutawl™, manufactured and sold only by the Cutawl Co., Route 6, Bethel, CT 06801. This unique tool is a precision cutting machine for all types of sheet materials, especially thin plyboards and Upson™ laminated fiberboards (Niagara Fiberboard, Inc., P.O. Box 828, Lockport, NY 14094).

No metal working tools will be needed. Nor are plastics used. The only conceivable use of metals would be in platforming, but facings and decor are simplified if wood is used throughout. As for thermoplastics, the vapors are extremely dangerous, and I suggest the purchase of needed items through display sources. See the chapter on "Props" for addresses.

Since so many of the "typical scenes" involve platforms, steps and ramps, a good place to start is with the 3/4" x 4 x 8 sheets of plywood which is basic to all elevated planes in the theatre and whose dimensions determine the design of pickup truck beds and the gate widths of vans and station wagons. We will also need about a gross of standard throat two-inch C-clamps (Adjustable #1420-2). This may seem like a lot but their use is legion, so get a good wholesale price through a church member in the supply business.

Note: The following lumber designations can be confusing. A 1 x 2 is actually 3/4" x 1-1/2" (used to be 1-5/8"), a 2 x 4 is now 1-1/2" x 3-1/3" (used to be 1-5/8" x 3-5/8") etc. However, the 3/4" (symbolized by 1) remains constant.

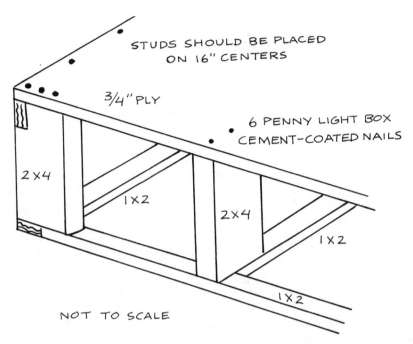

STUDS SHOULD BE PLACED
ON 16" CENTERS

3/4" PLY

6 PENNY LIGHT BOX
CEMENT-COATED NAILS

2×4

1×2

2×4

1×2

1×2

NOT TO SCALE

Let's begin with a simple and quick method of building a platform by a method of my own invention, which I call the *Stud* system. Let's construct a platform 18" high. We'll need some 2 x 4s and some 1 x 2s. Later, I'm going to recommend that the 1 x 2 strips be slightly wider, namely 1-13/16", which will involve ripping down 1 x 12s for a stock width useful for several other operations.

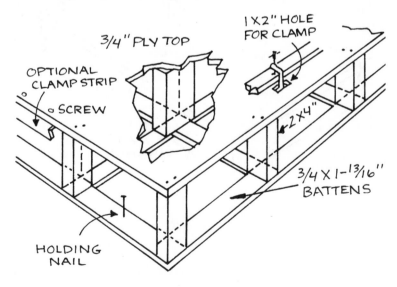

1X2" HOLE
FOR CLAMP

3/4" PLY TOP

OPTIONAL
CLAMP STRIP

SCREW

2×4"

3/4 × 1-13/16"
BATTENS

HOLDING
NAIL

23

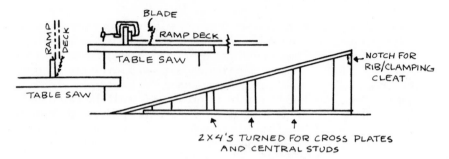

2 X 4'S TURNED FOR CROSS PLATES
AND CENTRAL STUDS

The 2 x 4s will be cut in lengths of 16-1/2" which allows for the thickness of the ply *plus* the thickness of the sill strips that will lock the 2 x 4s into a rigid structural system. This is accomplished by turning the 2 x 4s this way and that.

Also, with this technique, we are ready to construct the ramp. A table saw is essential in ripping the proper miters into the initial ramp deck.

Are there practical height limitations with the stud method of platform construction? Yes — at some point the weight of the forest of studs becomes onerous and potentially unstable. I would say the system works well with platforms not more than four feet high. Using some 2 x 6s at the corners will help. Of course, the interclamping of separate units increases rigidity considerably.

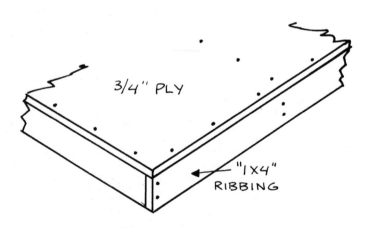

The illustration at the bottom of page 24 shows a simpler and more temporary method of building platforms. Three-quarter inch plywood panels can be strengthened by nailing on 1 x 4 ribbing. These can then be set on traditional sawhorses. This leaves the facing up for grabs, which can be accomplished by skirts of loose fabric "Velcroed" on. Adjacent platforms of the same height can be interclamped with the two-inch C-clamps which is a big plus over ribbing plywood sheets with heavier lumber. Once a ramp has been started (as above), clamped or bolted panels can be added. The whole sloped platform can be set on blocks.

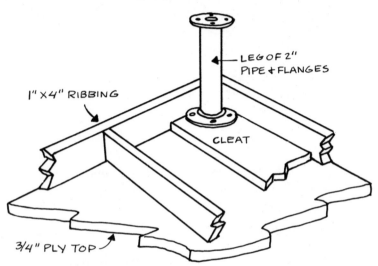

This reinforced type of platform top can be supported by pipe and flanges, especially where there are such obstacles as altar rails, etc. to overcome. However, pipe flanges and threadings are notoriously inaccurate and a lot of shimming is often necessary to level a platform. Again, this support method also leaves the facing up for grabs.

When it comes to steps and step runs I am completely wedded to another of my own designs, lap-jointed frames, using battens custom-ripped at 1-13/16" from soft pine 1 x 12s. This particular width was not determined in a haphazard manner. It has to do with the fact that 1 x 2s won't do for a reason I will discuss a little later on, and that 1 x 3s are too bulky. With the old 1 x 12s and a rip saw with a narrow kerf I would get six battens of equal width with the rip guide set to 1-13/16". Later, when the 1 x 12s "shrank," I liked the size so much I continued with it, using the narrower strip for braces, shoes, etc.

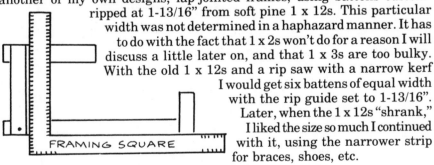

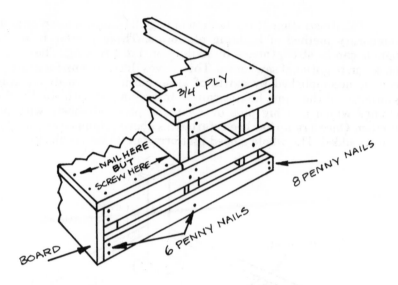

The above sketch will give you some idea of what we will be getting into: lightweight frames which are easily flush-surfaced by additional short batten pieces, and which can be clamped to other frames using the two-inch C-clamp.

Let's build a stair four feet wide with six-inch risers and twelve-inch treads. But first we must have a suitable working surface, for the lap-jointed frames will be secured with six-penny light box cement coated nails with the protruding ends later knocked over and hammered flat in the manner of cleats — these joints have got to hold! For this reason I use a soft pine work table top from which I pry up the completed frames prior to flattening the nail ends.

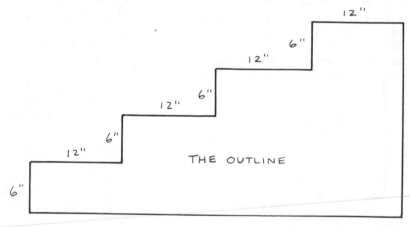

26

Here's how I go about making a step unit. Start with a large drawing of the outline like the one on the previous page. Full scale is recommended.

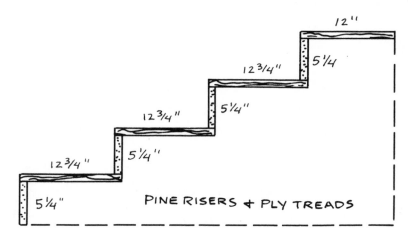

12"

12 3/4"   5 1/4

12 3/4"   5 1/4"

12 3/4"   5 1/4"

12 3/4"   5 1/4"

5 1/4"   PINE RISERS + PLY TREADS

Next, draw in the treads and risers. The treads will be cut from 3/4" plywood, the risers from 3/4" pine. Now draw in the horizontal and vertical battens as shown below.

HORIZONTAL + VERTICAL
BATTENS

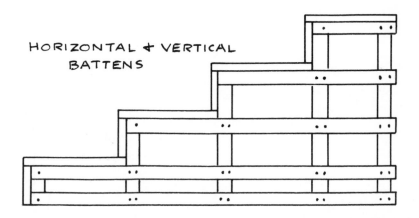

From this drawing a complete parts list can be made up similar to the one shown on the following page. Bear in mind that this step unit will be four feet wide, so three frames are needed, two on the outside and one on the inside. The outside frames will be built in reverse, so that the horizontals lie on the outside. This is to simplify facings. Note particularly the 3/4" holdbacks to the rear verticals for the outside frames, so that the verticals will not interfere with the 46-1/2" end pieces which will both join the frames and complete the flush structure for facing, when required.

PARTS LIST

48" treads: 3 — 12-3/4" wide; 1 — 12" wide
48" risers: 4 — 5-1/4" wide
(3/4" x 1-13/16" pine battens)

Horizontals:

4 — 3' 11-1/4"
2 — 3' 10-1/2" (center frame)
2 — 2' 11-1/4"
1 — 2' 10-1/2" (center frame)
2 — 1' 11-1/4"
1 — 1' 10-1/2" (center frame)
2 — 11-1/4"
1 — 10-1/2" (center frame)

Verticals:

6 — 1' 11-1/4"
3 — 1' 5-1/4"
3 — 11-1/4"
3 — 5-1/4"

Ends:

3 — 46-1/2"

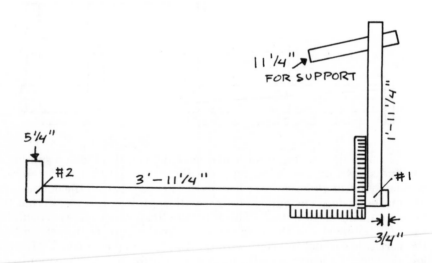

Now start a frame. Lay down the bottom horizontal. Place the end vertical on top, using the top horizontal loosely laid under for support. Offset (hold back) the vertical 3/4" from the end, square up and drive in one six-penny cement coated nail. Now go to the other end and drive in another nail. The horizontal is now locked to the worktable. Checking the square carefully, drive in another nail at each end. Now assemble all the parts, checking your drawing to be sure exactly where the verticals go and where the horizontals take off from the end vertical. Accuracy is essential. Now pull up the frame and bend over nail ends that are sticking out. Remember to make the other outside frame *reversed*. The inside frame can be made any way.

Assemble the step unit by setting the treads in place and nailing into the frames below, a few nails here and there at first until you are sure the alignment is correct. Now slip in the risers. It is best to screw up into risers from below because this will be the weakest connection. The risers can be nailed in from above. Now slip in the center frame and secure. Add the end horizontals. If the step unit is a high one you may want to add a diagonal in place of the middle end horizontal. If the unit is to be covered, short batten scraps can be added to the rear verticals to flush up the surface.

Now I realize that all this may sound complicated, but I go through the full scale drawing and same sort of parts list for every step unit I build, otherwise I would get completely mixed up. When you have finally assembled your first step unit you will see the logic to it. The unit is lightweight, amazingly strong, and compatible with all my stagecraft systems. It will be one of the first pieces borrowed. In reassembling platform sets I have built in the past I often have to run all over town rounding up the parts.

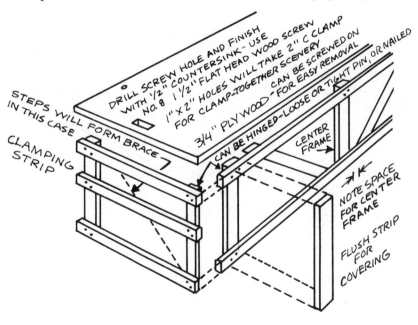

Platforms can be made in much the same way, though the frames are usually disassembled for storage. Even when the frames are only lightly nailed (not cross-nailed) they are incredibly stable. When you start clamping them to each other, and add step units as well, stability turns into rigidity of the highest order.

I have developed a simple and very effective way to construct scenery for houses, walls, etc. that feature embrasures. I call it the *Slab* system, using the same 3/4" x 1-13/16" battens turned on edge. Not only is a believable thickness achieved but the structures are load bearing.

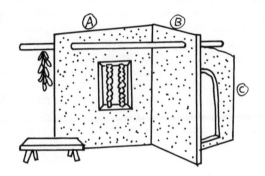

The detail drawing shows the clamping potential, using the stand two-inch C-clamp. It also shows that the batten must be at least 1-3/4" wide, otherwise the hook end of the clamp cannot be accommodated.

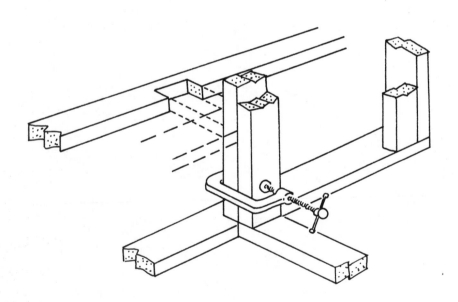

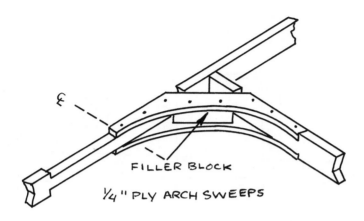

FILLER BLOCK

¼" PLY ARCH SWEEPS

The filler block is to maintain the proper separation of the sweeps during covering. If the slab frame is to support weight, the filler block should be lengthened and serve as a brace. The cutting of the notches is best accomplished with a band saw. The frames for the tomb scene in Chapter 2 can be developed in this manner.

On the following page a rear view of the complete frame for (A) slab panel is shown. A plus for the slab system of construction is that all faces are flush and can be covered if sight lines require it. The same is true for the ramp, step and platform construction previously shown.

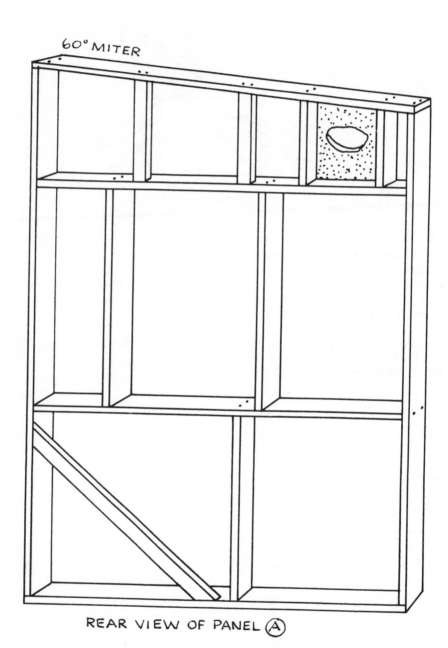

60° MITER

REAR VIEW OF PANEL Ⓐ

The above facade is constructed in the same slab manner and helps form a pavilion with an upper acting deck. However, it is the construction of the stair units to the rear which merits close examination: a method of interconnecting hollowed-out trapezoidal shafts or *piers*. Disassembled, the piers pack well for storage and transportation. Assembled, the structural rigidity is astounding. Furthermore, piers can be switched to form a serpentine or double curve in a tight situation.

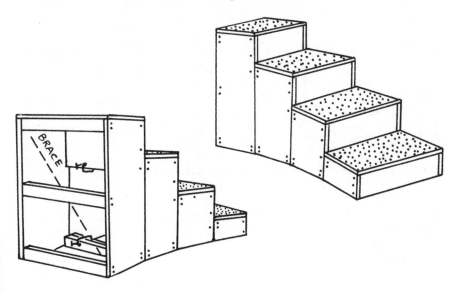

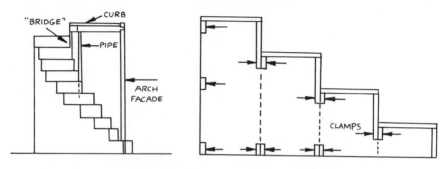

The initial pavilion with two sets of steps was built for the Everyman Players' national tour of *Pilgrim's Progress*. I added a third stair unit when I used the pavilion later in another church production. And portions of the stairs I have used ever since whenever I need a quick stair, especially since the clamping is compatible with other structures that I build.

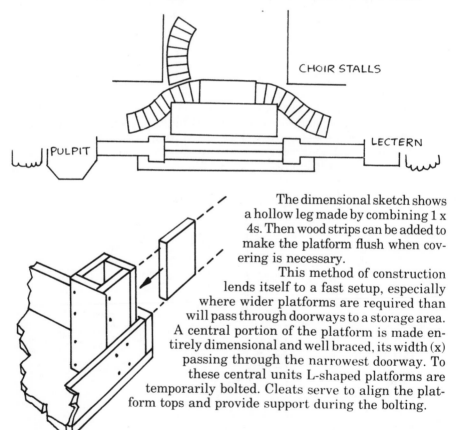

The dimensional sketch shows a hollow leg made by combining 1 x 4s. Then wood strips can be added to make the platform flush when covering is necessary.

This method of construction lends itself to a fast setup, especially where wider platforms are required than will pass through doorways to a storage area. A central portion of the platform is made entirely dimensional and well braced, its width (x) passing through the narrowest doorway. To these central units L-shaped platforms are temporarily bolted. Cleats serve to align the platform tops and provide support during the bolting.

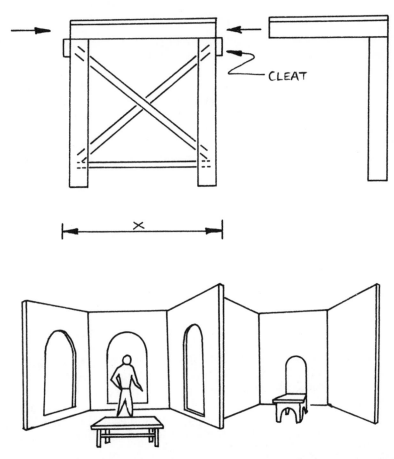

In this sketch you are looking at a set of archway panel threefolds, and a set of plain folding panels. All these panels have completely reversible cloth flap hinging (similar to fabric covered rudders and ailerons on light aircraft, not to mention many children's folding toys). The advantage of this method of hinging is twofold: complete flexibility of positioning and the absence of an "open" joint such as results from hinges which revolve about a pin. Unfortunately, this hinging method requires frames that are flush on both sides!

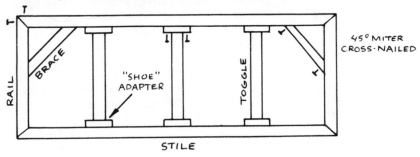

Building a frame like the one on page 35 that is flush on both sides means giving up a conventional method of framing up scenery: the tacking on of thin strips of plywood over the joints, pieces variously called corner blocks, keystones, straps or gussets. Unless one has the equipment for mortise and tenon joints, this means mitering the corners and cross-nailing, and fitting "shoe" adapters to the toggles. In all this, a drill to make some feeler holes will keep the wood from splitting. I like to screw in the braces to avoid a diagonal hammer thrust which might knock a frame out of kilter. After sanding the sharp exterior edges the frame can be covered on both sides with muslin.

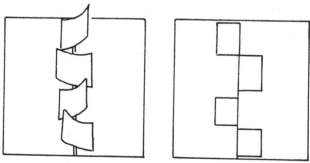

To understand reversible cloth flap hinging, take a couple of pieces of cardboard and lay them side by side. Cut some pieces of paper and glue one half of each piece alternately as shown, the first piece to the cardboard on the right side, the next piece to the cardboard on the left side, and so on. When these are dry turn the pieces over and glue the free ends down in such a way that the cardboard pieces are locked together. The cardboard pieces can now be folded in either direction.

The model clearly shows that if the hinge flaps touch they will fray; otherwise they should be as close as possible. And upon folding the cardboard parts you will notice that the flaps do not conceal all the raw edges. Fold them one way and you see some raw edges. Fold them the other way and you see other raw edges. If the frames of a screen are completely covered with muslin and then flap hinged with muslin after which the whole is painted, this problem disappears. But if you are using dyed fabrics and the hinge flaps go down first, with the covering fabric stapled down later, you will have to cut open sleeves of the same fabric to conceal all the edges to be hinged before you begin.

The interesting thing about this hinged joint is that the joint seems to disappear to all but the most critical observer — a far cry from joints with metal hinges where an open crack is inevitable in a certain position.

Other fabrics can be used for folding screens. One such fabric is Veltex™, a teasled velour (Valley Forge Fabrics, New York). Veltex comes in a fifty-four inch width so the frames can be forty inches wide. Cover one side completely, taking the cloth around the edges and finishing up on the rear. The hinge flaps are placed face down on the finished side and

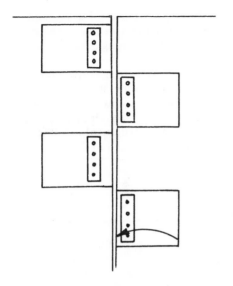

small strips of mat board are tacked on. Turn the frames over and fish the ends up. In the upholstery trade this is known as "blind tacking." The rear side can now be covered, trimming and turning under the excess cloth where necessary. On the rear the staples will show, so rub the sticks of staples with magic marker to make them less visible.

The best fabric for freestanding scenery in the church is burlap, especially dyed burlap. Because of its rich texture, burlap has always responded well to any kind of directional lighting, and its texture is particularly compatible with architectural surfaces. Its rough texture also lends itself to "drybrushing," a technique discussed in Chapter 5, one by which suggestive detail is added to an existing surface with a minimal amount of paint. However, getting burlap in place on our scenery, especially on folding screens, requires careful, disciplined work.

In the first place, burlap is visibly porous — not only can you often see through it if a brighter light source lies beyond it, but also the bare wood of the scenic frames shows through. Therefore, some sort of liner is required. I have used two layers of 60 lb. kraft paper, sprayed with flame retardant.

Burlap is held in place by staples, and since a considerable number of these staples will be on the face of the scenery, they must be of a light enough gauge to nearly camouflage their presence by sinking into the rough burlap texture. They must also be long enough to pass through several layers of the fabric, yet must be easily removable when fabrics are stretched or replaced. The 5/16" staple is satisfactory. The Swingline 101™ stapler is easier on the hand than the Arrow JT-21™. Automatic staplers are not very useful because this is a precision operation. Before we get into burlap covering, however, with "slab" constructed scenery the natural thickness of the 1-13/16" framing must be "open sleeved" with burlap strips, especially around openings or curved surfaces where the burlap cannot be pulled around.

When hinging and covering a set of plain folding screens, the edges to be hinged must first be open sleeved with long narrow strips of burlap. Then the frames are laid side by side and the hinge flaps stapled down in an alternating pattern as in our little cardboard model.

When covering, start with a selvage edge about 1/16th of an inch back from the edge of the frame where hinged. Then bring the burlap

37

around the other edge and staple to the rear. Turn the burlap under at the top and bottom, creasing the edges. Some panels will be in the middle of a multiple folding screen so you will have to turn a long edge under also.

If the tensions are correct the burlap should lie as tautly as the blanket on an army cot during basic training. When sags develop in time, the material can be restretched after removing some staples.

Sooner or later we come to the flat-framed archway, not as simply constructed as the "slab" archway. I use a series of arch sweeps mainly to keep the unit lightweight yet maintain some structural integrity. The method shown is load-bearing — I chin myself on each arch frame I complete.

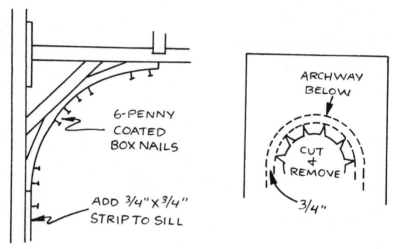

Above left is a typical arch construction. To the right is the method by which archways are covered on one side, with the burlap pulled around. On the other side excess material is tucked under. To save burlap, use wide strips from below the arch to the sill.

Sills are essential to all freestanding scenery. There is no problem with sills for slab scenery but on flat-folding scenery I reduce that portion of the bottom rail in an archway or doorway to 1-3/4" in height. When sills reach to the frame's exterior the sill piece can be halve-jointed (rabbeted) into the stiles. On all sills the burlap can be attached with a thin layer of Elmer's™ glue, then trimmed when dry.

For curved scenic surfaces bend Easy Curve™ Upson Fiberboard frames such as shown at right. Easy Curve is manufactured by Niagara Fiberboard, Inc., P.O. Box 828, Lockport, NY 14094. Write for a catalog or phone (716) 434-8881 for a distributor nearest you.

To construct a portion of a curved wall you must first make a full scale paper pattern which will include the location of the stiles. Cut the top and bottom arcs, transferring the data from the paper pattern, showing both the stile locations and the identification of the pine horizontal segments. Now remove the stile locations from the paper pattern and use the remaining pieces for tracing onto pine the horizontal segments A', B' and C'. Assemble as shown. You will have to glue the top and bottom pine segments to the plywood arcs.

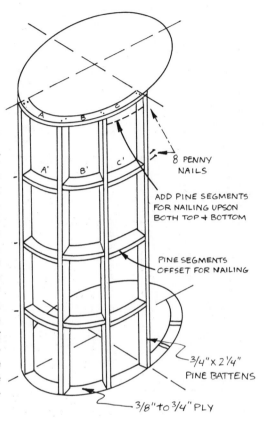

8 PENNY NAILS

ADD PINE SEGMENTS FOR NAILING UPSON BOTH TOP + BOTTOM

PINE SEGMENTS OFFSET FOR NAILING

3/4" x 2 1/4" PINE BATTENS

3/8" to 3/4" PLY

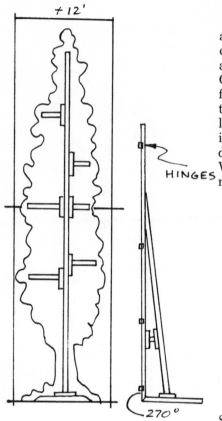

+ 12'

HINGES

270°

In conjunction with the Cutawl, all sorts of foliage and profile cutouts can be made on Pebbled Upsonite™, a heavier stock than Easy Curve. Once the Upsonite is profiled, a framework of light battens can be attached to the rear. Coat the battens lightly with Elmer's glue; while drying, hold them in place by light nails driven though to a soft worktable. When the glue has set, pull out the nails and prepare the brace jacks.

Several panels of this sort can be cloth flap hinged for flexible positioning, self-support, and compact storage.

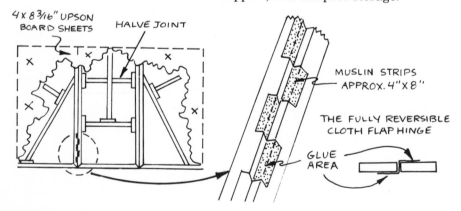

4 X 8 ³⁄₁₆" UPSON BOARD SHEETS

HALVE JOINT

MUSLIN STRIPS
APPROX. 4" X 8"

THE FULLY REVERSIBLE
CLOTH FLAP HINGE

GLUE
AREA

While no longer easily found, try to get hold of some porch-type rolling blinds made of wooden slats. Make these into woodland profiles as shown in the sketch. They can be painted or, better yet, cut narrow strips of dyed felt and glue them on the slats creating a dazzling mosaic of nature's embroidery. These serpentines can also be wound about columns.

SOME LATERAL BINDERS MUST BE TIED OFF

WOODEN DISK

PLAN

Chapter 4:

The Finding or Making of Props

To a layman, "props" is an all-inclusive term denoting everything on the stage other than the actors. In theatrical lingo, however, "props" are that miscellany of items ranging from smoke and foodstuff to loose furniture and tablecloths — in effect, everything *but* scenery. Sketched above is an overly enthusiastic cleric swinging a censer with an especially "oily" brand of incense!

The prop master is that genius who knows what to collect from rummage sales, antique emporiums and such, hiding his treasures in a dusty attic against that rainy day when just the right props can literally make an entire scene.

For reference, the prop master should have for handy reference copies of the display magazine *Visual Merchandising*, 407 Gilbert Ave., Cincinnati, OH 45202, the current *Theatre Crafts Directory*, Theatre Crafts Magazine, 135 Fifth Ave., New York, NY 10010, and the *Source Book Directory* of Exhibit Builder Magazine, P.O. Box 4144, Woodland Hills, CA 91365.

From these publications the prop master can find his way to sources from which hard-to-find artifacts can be purchased. For safety's sake, one should avoid the fabrication of props involving the urethane foams, etc. These chemicals can prove lethal from prolonged inhalation of vapors and contact with the skin.

It is a general rule that any furniture which you can make will appear more convincing because it can be scaled down from actual size — a technique Disney Studios use, including buildings themselves. This is especially true with freestanding scenery when a literal illusion is not sought.

Shown upside-down is a portion of a refectory table. The table top can be thickened by adding strips of 1 x 2s or our customary batten around the edge on the underside, and the table ends can be doubled. Use a band saw to prepare the stretcher tongues and a drill and saber saw for the wedge holes.

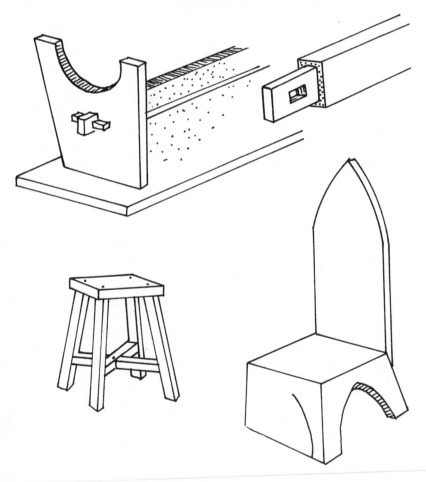

Design a chair as if it were a box. The Cutawl has a blade for profiling intricate designs in 3/4" plywood. Stools and benches are a must. A bench can be a miniaturized version of the stretcher table.

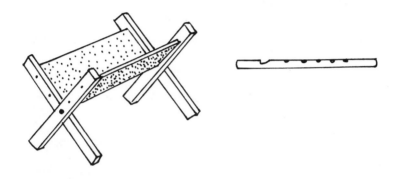

Make a manger from a sawhorse, a flute from a simple dowel.

As I remarked earlier, a ramped acting platform makes a powerful visual statement. However, a decision must be made whether or not to fit the scenery and props to the slope. In the era of permanently sloped stages the scenery was not a problem because most of it consisted of flats running laterally in grooves both above and below. But when I designed the *Dybbuk* for a nine-degree triangular sloped stage the threefold set piece shown had to be adjusted for that particular position (and it remained useless thereafter). I also customized the bema and all furniture props.

One of my favorite scenes in terms of a highly dramatic visual image involved a banquet scene on a large ramped platform. (See illustration on page 46.) The actors sat Oriental style on the floor along each side of a long trestle table, itself ramped and truncated. The table was structurally sound since some of the actors had to walk on it.

A most useful prop is a hand-carried lantern.

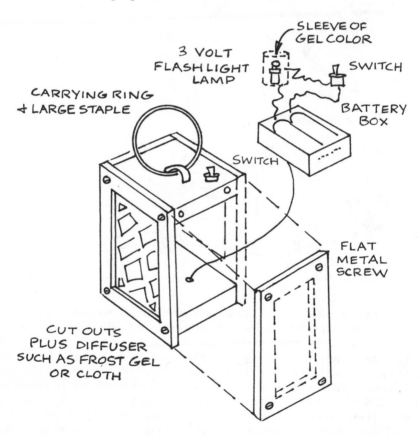

SLEEVE OF GEL COLOR

3 VOLT FLASHLIGHT LAMP

SWITCH

CARRYING RING + LARGE STAPLE

BATTERY BOX

SWITCH

FLAT METAL SCREW

CUT OUTS PLUS DIFFUSER SUCH AS FROST GEL OR CLOTH

Start with two nine-inch squares of 3/4" soft pine to form the base and top. From Upsonite or other lightweight panel board cut the face plates as follows: two 9" x 12" and two 9+" x 12" as shown. Secure either thin white cloth or diffusion "gels" to the rear. Three of these panels can be secured permanently and will form the structure of the lantern. The fourth should be removable to service the lamp and batteries.

Build a little box to contain the two flashlight batteries in such a way that you can jam the batteries against the metal contact strips which you have fashioned from tin can stock. Wire the batteries in series. Solder wires to a three-volt flashlight lamp and intercept the circuit with a switch. A small sleeve or cylinder of plastic "gel" around the lamp will provide the color.

Chapter 5:

Painting Scenery

I first became aware of the nature of picture frames when I was in prep school. Along the walls of the corridor leading to the dining hall were hung massive paintings depicting scenes from King Arthur's world, paintings framed in heavy oak and bearing brass plaques honoring grateful alumni.

When I grew older and went to college, I began noticing that the more literal a painting the heavier and more ornate the frame — the Hudson River landscapes, for example; the more abstract or suggestive the painting, the less frame there was — and in some cases, none at all!

When later I came to "space staging," I realized I had fallen into a situation in which the absence of a strong frame such as a proscenium virtually dictated a non-pictorial approach to scene painting.

Right off, here are two general rules which will help.

Rule One: If the scenery is a set of folding panels — rectangular for the convenience of self-support if for nothing else — detailed imagery should taper off well before reaching the edges of the panels. If a dyed fabric base is used, preferably a textured one such as burlap, the color and texture will carry the eye through the transition of the joint.

Rule Two: When the profile (silhouette) of a scenic piece is a strong one, such as a distinctive building shape or trees and foliage whose outlines are heavily scrolled by the Cutawl, then detailed imagery *can* be brought to the edges.

At first glance, these rules appear contradictory; actually they are not, for in the latter instance the heavily profiled silhouette is very much a space separator which prevents the detailed painting from direct contact with the environment around it.

There are many factors to consider in scene painting: the talent pool, the materials involved, and the long-term use of the artifacts created. Ask yourself, "Do I have a consummate brush artist or a tyro who can handle stencils, a spray gun and little else? Do I want 'drybrush' on burlap for the sake of a rich texture, or will an ample use of dyed fabric and a miscellany of props such as lanterns, shutters, etc. require no further detailing?"

Let's begin with two walls of a partial house, as shown in the illustration on page 51. The two frames are covered with a heavy grade of raw burlap, then hinged together to become self-supporting. Concealed by the twofold is a piece of 3/4" plywood, sandbagged, to which the twofold is loose-pin hinged. Segments of a rug roll, sprayed terra cotta and shaded by magic marker, provide the roof tiles.

A prop lantern hangs from a bracket bolted to the wall. The supporting line passing through a pulley contains the electrical circuit. Lath strips form the upper part of the open window. Behind the window is tacked an off-white cloth which can be lit by a small floodlight mounted below eye level. The lantern and the floodlit window are important because they will "spark" the scene.

The shutters and window ledge are faked, created by spraying through stencils cut from cardboard. Likewise, the bush is created by spraying through stencils. When a soft-edged effect is desired, hold the stencil slightly away from the surface.

The tree is a plywood profile with green burlap adhered by a thin coat of Elmer's glue. And last, both the house and the tree are shaded with a darker color by means of a spray gun. No paint brush and very little paint has been used.

BURLAP GLUED ONTO
PROFILED PLYWOOD
THEN SHADED BY SPRAY

SHADING ON SECTIONS
OF RUG ROLL

CARDBOARD
STENCILS
PLUS
LATH STRIPS

SHADING BY
SPRAY GUN

GROUND ROW

CARDBOARD
STENCILS

There are two grades of denim, one used primarily for work clothes, another of fine quality used for covering cushions and furniture. This grade is also useful for scenery — it is sufficiently nubby to have a good texture and rugged enough for reversible cloth flap hinging. Because of the manner in which it is woven the reverse side has a different look.

Nowadays most scene painting is done with acrylic latex paints. My advice to the reader is to use brands which are sold by scenic houses rather than those bought at local paint stores. The difference has to do with quality; scenic paints are made with purer colors and intermix well, while other brands "muddy" when mixed. One notable exception is Pittsburgh℠ paints, which has an excellent acrylic latex decorator line.

This is not to say the old dry colors mixed with glue and casein binders are obsolete — if you have some of these powders you can mix them with acrylic latex white for additional touch-up and detailing.

However, the primary thrust of this chapter is "drybrush" painting on burlap, both natural and dyed, for this results in an imagery which carries us as far as possible from the sort of pictorialism that is definitely out of place in the architectural ambience of the church.

By "drybrushing" is meant the depositing of paint on the outer nap of the fabric only, a technique which will require some practice. The basic brushes will be a one-inch and a two-inch scenic liner, these of good quality from a scenic supply house, and a one and one-half inch very worn out, stubby, ordinary paint brush. You will need some flat pie tins for three functions: a brush can be dipped on its side, a brush can be wiped off flat and evenly, and the pie tin can be used as a mixing palette.

Let's do a plaster wall with some occasional bricks showing through. For plaster walls on natural burlap, make the highlighted areas, suggesting slightly raised portions of the plaster, with the two-inch liner, dipped in creamy beige paint. On eggshell burlap, use white paint. Hold the brush at about thirty degrees and glide onto and off the surface in much the same way as an airplane pilot practices continuous landings and takeoffs, thus creating feather edges. Every effort must be made to keep the point on the outer fibers of the burlap only, avoiding complete saturation. Strokes can go in many directions.

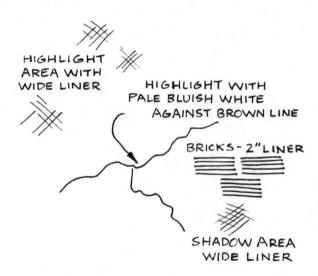

HIGHLIGHT
AREA WITH
WIDE LINER

HIGHLIGHT WITH
PALE BLUISH WHITE
AGAINST BROWN LINE

BRICKS - 2" LINER

SHADOW AREA
WIDE LINER

Develop highlights further by changing pressure during the stroke or varying the amount of paint on the brush. Shadowing is done the same way as highlighting using bluish brown. Areas where the plaster has peeled away are also shadowed. Lath below plaster will cause the plaster to be stained brown. Bricks produce an orange stain. Complete the detailing by marking a greater portion of the crack line with bluish white. Learn how to do only a portion of the plaster wall in complete detail, and continue by highlighting and shadowing beyond this area, ever less precisely. In this manner the majority of the surface need not be detailed, but is suggested. Finish by lightly brushing a trace of yellow across some of the highlighting.

With bricks use the two-inch flat lining brush and make each brick length one stroke only. Start with dark orange-red or brown. Mix white into brick tones. Accent with brighter orange or pink-orange. Allow some bricks to fade away as if still covered with plaster. Lay in bricks in plastered areas to suggest they have "bled" through by mixing white into the brick tones. For mortar between bricks, shadow with dark blue-gray, using the one-inch liner. *Do not outline* more than a few of the bricks, but merely suggest the mortar occasionally.

Lightly draw in the pattern of the stones in a stone wall with chalk. Use the two-inch liner dipped in bluish-gray paint to stroke in the shadow facets on the surface of the rock. Choose one or two facets on each stone and lightly stroke in the highlights with light gray paint on natural burlap or white paint on eggshell burlap. Use the one-inch liner with dark gray-blue to suggest the cracks between the stones, but *do not outline* every stone.

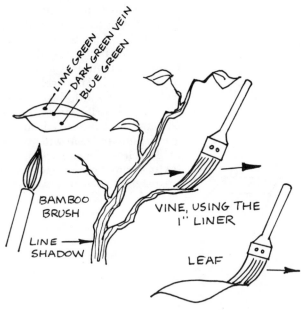

For vines, hold the one-inch lining brush nearly perpendicular to the painting surface with the narrow side leading. Use greens and browns. Paint in the direction in which things grow. Let the ends of the vine trail away to nothing. Press down hard on the brush and also rotate slightly for the flat part of the leaf. Return to the thin line position. Use a pointed brush for small details such as leaf veins or highlights and shadows. A slight touch of yellow will make the leaf appear more lifelike.

The foregoing instructions for drybrush painting are taken verbatim from notes Irene Corey gave me. Her colors included acrylic latex White, Yellow Ochre, Raw Sienna, Burnt Sienna, Fire Red, Venetian Red, Thalo Green, Ultramarine Blue and Black, and an assortment of the old pigments plus pastel chalks and Craypas℠ (with clear plastic spray).

Irene did not usually work on burlap. She painted for me because I built a lot of scenery for the Everyman Players and she was the principal designer. I used burlap for the reasons I have already given and she knew how to handle it. I was lucky to have her for I am not a good brush artist.

Another time I had the services of a quite different brush artist, Drew Hunter. His favorite painting surface was the smooth side of Masonite℠ sheets — for fast brush action. However, his quasi-pictorial style worked well for me because his Masonite panels were beautifully profiled, a design form which also works well in space staging.

So there you have it — a wide range of techniques from textured Pointillism to a highly profiled Pictorialism, each artist contributing in his own way to freestanding imagery.

I have always built as many furniture props as possible, believing that a reduction in scale plus a certain homemade look enhanced my settings, and in the painting of these I developed a style of my own — a

basic coat quickly overlaid with partially drybrush colors which blended into the prime color in varying degrees depending upon the amount of added paint and the drying speed. This technique also works well on tree and foliage profiles.

Dyed burlap started out life as brownish jute. So while dyed burlaps may look great, light and heat will gradually do them in. To refresh faded burlap, sponge into the texture some grocery store dyes as close to the original color as possible.

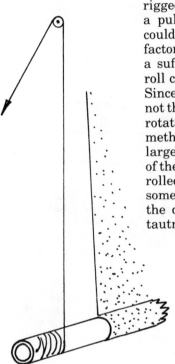

This sketch shows how a roll drop is rigged. The purchase line passes through a pulley and ends on the roller, which could well be a cardboard tube from a rug factory. When the purchase line is pulled, a sufficient number of turns around the roll causes the roll to "walk up the drop." Since the fabric is supporting the tube and not the line, which is only making the tube rotate, there is no sagging. This is a good method by which to allow a tapestry or large scroll to be dropped into the space of the church. When the drop is completely rolled up it will have disappeared behind some architectural header. Note also that the drop should be tapered to maintain tautness along the sides.

Chapter 6:

Lighting the Church Play

FOLLOW SPOT
ON STAND

EXTENSION
CORDS

HOMEMADE
LIGHT STANDS
AND SPOTS

DIMMERS

The most practical approach to lighting a church play is that of "overlighting," that is, by adding "highlights" to appropriate portions of the existing sanctuary illumination. Attempting to light from scratch with portable equipment isn't practical: proper mounting positions are scarce; connecting a dimmer bank of that capacity to a central power source can be difficult (and should be done by a licensed electrician); and there will be a goodly number of unsightly cables strung about.

The above sketch will give you some idea of what's needed: lightweight spotlight stands, extension cords, some small dimmers and a theatrical quality spotlight with iris control on a short stand.

With basic manual arts tools, a skillful scenery designer can take advantage of the do-it-yourself home building centers and mill ends discount fabric outlets. But theatrical lighting is different, for while there are plenty of parts for simple floodlights on the hardware store shelves, certain items such as dimmers and adjustable spotlights must be purchased outright.

However, before proceeding further I will have to decide whether it is best to identify some key items by specific name, source and approximate cost, thus risking having the information being out-of-date possibly before publication, or playing it safe by talking about things in general terms, which equates with vagueness as far as some readers are concerned. I have decided to take the riskier course and name a few names.

You will need to make a survey of all available wall outlets (also known as "convenience receptacles," usually duplex). By code, these are circuited through 20-ampere breakers or fuses though you may find some fused at 15 amperes, especially in older installations. Several receptacles may be grouped on one fused circuit and it will be your job to find out which! For this survey you will need the help of another worker, one to plug in some sort of lamp, the other to turn the circuits off and on. Generally, in public buildings, opposite sides of a large room (the nave, for instance) are separate circuits. The narthex or lobby receptacles are usually separately circuited, as are lectern, pulpit and choir areas.

Be wary of equipment that might be added to supposedly "free" circuits! I once placed a follow spot on a small balcony above the lobby of a small rural church. Though I had made my survey on a quiet afternoon I overlooked a coke machine half hidden in a corner of the lobby below. When the parishioners arrived for the program I was aghast to hear bottles clanking and I realized the motor was draining away my power. The only other free circuit I had found was attached to a drop cord in the minister's office, to which the mimeograph machine was attached. Fortunately that machine was not needed during the evening!

It is also amazing how many times some deacon, trying to be helpful, starts rearranging the lighting ambience you have carefully worked out in conjunction with portable dimmers, turning off, in the process, some of the receptacles into which you have plugged your dimmers. If you have the personnel to spare, I suggest posting a guard by the circuit breaker panel — it's usually located well out of sight in some obscure closet or corridor.

The subject of theatrical dimming is a complex one, thus often confusing to the layman. The simplest form of all dimming is that of resistance (a rheostat) where an adjustable resistor is so constructed that its resistance may be changed without opening the circuit. It might be likened to an adjustable toaster because the unwanted current is drawn off in heat, or, in a water analogy, the cutting of holes in a garden hose to prevent the full pressure from reaching the nozzle. Today resistance dimming, once necessary for direct current, has been largely superseded, but the principle would be quite satisfactory for our needs here.

With the advent of alternating current the most reliable dimmer has been the autotransformer. Simply stated, an autotransformer dimmer is one which has a single winding around a silicon steel core. A mechanical slider passes over an exposed portion of the winding, tapping off the voltage desired. A water analogy would be decreasing the flow of water by turning the faucet. Although an autotransformer is a heavy object and basically a manual controller, it is inherently silent and free of radio interference, important points when you consider the portable dimmers are often right in the audience and adjacent to portable sound equipment.

Another type of dimmer is the silicon controlled rectifier, consisting of a pair of rectifiers, one for each half-cycle of the alternating current. The "SCR" is basically a switching device. A transistorized pilot circuit controls the length of time the switch is open during the "on" period of each rectifier. In a water analogy each of the pair of recitifiers may be said to produce spurts of water, the duration of the spurts being variable.

The analogy also points up the fact that the "SCR" operates by "chopping" into the characteristic wave pattern of alternating current. This "chopping," unless smoothed out by proper filters, chokes and capacitors, produces *radio frequency interference* and *lamp sing*, that is, sound interference and mechanical vibrations in lamp filaments. The chief advantage of "SCR" dimming is the simplicity of low voltage remote controllers which, when hooked to electronic memory systems, eliminate the old handwritten cue sheets and, in large installations, even the cumbersome "patch" panels for the grouping of circuitry. Also, the low voltage control wires can be freely strung about, thus making the remote control of separately located light stands possible.

There are some factors to be considered on the down side of electronic dimming. First, there is an inherent voltage drop over full line voltage. This is caused by the various filters, chokes and capacitators which "smooth" wave forms distortion. About three per cent of full line voltage is lost and the color temperature and candlepower specified for lamp filaments are not achieved. Of course, this drop could be compensated by booster transformers but this is not economically viable in a competitive market. In large installations this drop can be offset somewhat by adding more lighting units. But in our "Poor Richard" operation every bit of brilliance is important.

Second, there is no way to walk around the cost of a properly filtered electronic dimmer. Off-the-shelf hardware store dimmers for home lighting fixtures are not reliable unless permanently wired into a circuit. Plugging fixtures into such a dimmer that is already turned on (known as "hot patching" in the theatrical trade) will usually cause the dimmer to fail (and, by the way, this is also true of autotransformer dimmers, which damages the coil contacts). Further, these little dimmers can create static which feeds back into sound equipment. Try using your cordless telephone with your dining room chandelier turned on, or plug a radio into a nearby outlet.

TYPICAL PORTABLE WALL OUTLET
DIMMER HOOKUPS

SCR DIMMER UNIT

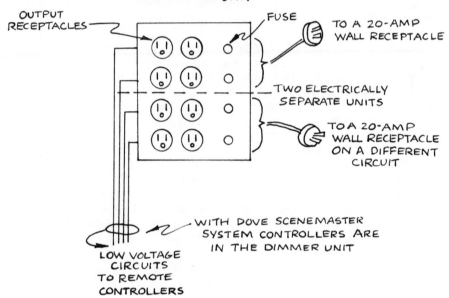

OUTPUT RECEPTACLES

FUSE

TO A 20-AMP WALL RECEPTACLE

TWO ELECTRICALLY SEPARATE UNITS

TO A 20-AMP WALL RECEPTACLE ON A DIFFERENT CIRCUIT

WITH DOVE SCENEMASTER SYSTEM CONTROLLERS ARE IN THE DIMMER UNIT

LOW VOLTAGE CIRCUITS TO REMOTE CONTROLLERS

Given these reservations, there are some properly filtered electronic systems that are designed for the 20-amp wall outlet hookup method. While one hesitates to list sources in a manual that might just outlast specific manufacturers in a volatile marketplace, I'll give several that are valid for 1989: Dove Systems of San Luis Obispo, California, particularly the Scenemaster I™ with 1000-watt dimmers; LSS Laboratories of Wallingford, Connecticut with their M-3000 dimmer pack designed for small bands and clubs; and Grand Stage Co. of Chicago, Illinois with their Warrior 412™ and Procon II™ Control Console.

When autotransformer dimmers were plentiful the dial types could be built into small wooden carrying cases and items such as fuses, output receptacles, plugs, cords and wires added from readily available shelf items

60

in local building supply stores. There are still some stockpiles of dimmers used in the repair of autotransformer dimmers. Contact Vara-Light/Dimmatronics of Crystal Lake, Illinois.

Superior Electric Co. of Bristol, Connecticut still manufactures wall box dimmers for commercial installations such as restaurants, etc. The 800-watt (for use with a 750-watt followspot) and the 1800-watt units are useful. Below is the 1800-watt unit boxed for travel and showing my own arrangement of additional circuitry.

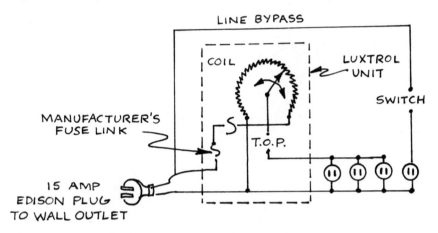

For individual use such as we are doing here it doesn't matter which way the plug is inserted in a wall outlet. But if you were installing this unit in a building you would follow instructions and identify the hot and neutral wires.

"S" is a switch which opens when the knob is turned all the way down. "T.O.P." is a thermal overload protector which cycles off-and-on to warn of overloads.

The illustration on the following page shows the Superior 1800-watt wall box dimmer mounted to 1/2" plywood which is recessed against 3/4" x 4" cleats.

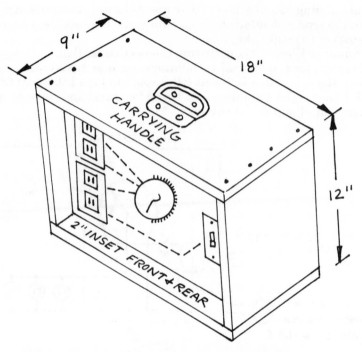

In addition to Superior Electric, the old VARIAC℠ adjustable auto-transformers are now manufactured by Technipower of Danbury, Connecticut. These are designed chiefly for laboratory use and are individually packaged, complete with output receptacle, input cable and plug, and a protective fusing. All in all, allow about $1,000 for dimming needs, including homemade cases and parts.

There is one other essential piece of equipment which must be pur-

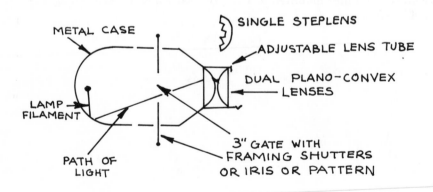

chased outright and which is rather expensive: a theatrical quality adjustable ellipsoidal reflector spotlight with iris control. An ellipsoidal spotlight is a precision optical instrument. With the help of an ellipsoidal shaped reflector of polished aluminum (Alzak) the output from a carefully positioned lamp passes through a focal plane about three inches in diameter called the "gate" where the beam can be shaped by framing shutters or an iris, or patterned by silhouette inserts. Then the light passes through a lens system.

While there is a variety of ellipsoidal spotlights for a wide range of tasks, our need is for an operator manned spotlight which can be subtly directed towards points of interest, adding a concentration of brilliance on top of our specialized floodlighting which supplements a low level of overall church illumination. And when I say "subtle" I mean just that: with the proper manipulation of direction, the iris and a dimmer, the operator should be able to add brilliance without the audience being aware of such adjustments.

The ellipsoidal spotlight is a projector of sorts and can be had with a pattern slot where a design template may be inserted. Of late, stainless steel mats are available into which artwork can be etched. In addition, there are literally hundreds of currently available patterns ranging from stained glass windows to stars. Check your Theatre Crafts Directory for The Great American Market and Rosco Laboratories.

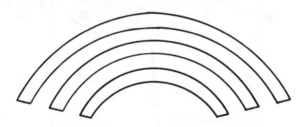

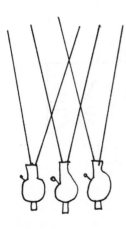

The rainbow for Noah's Ark is perhaps one of the most difficult effects in a church space. An obvious solution is projection but equipment for this effect is either space-consuming or expensive. However, there is a compact solution: three custom-made patterns for three separate ellipsoidal spotlights, each "gelled" with a different color.

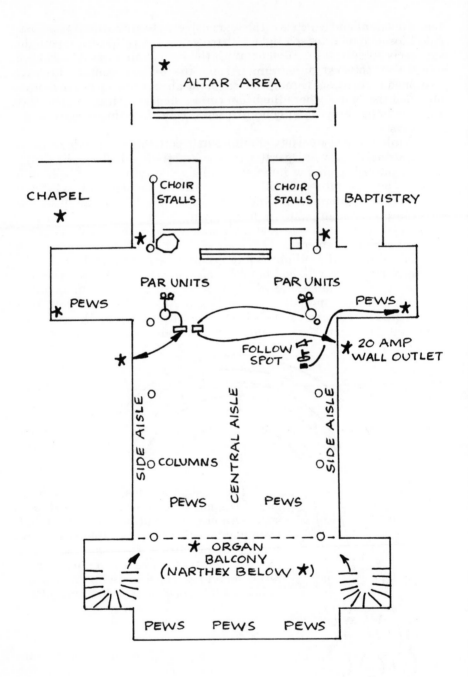

In the rough church diagram of a supplementary electrical layout, I show one follow spot location close in, in the partial protection of a nave colonnade. Here we could probably get by with a 500-watt six-inch ellipsoidal with two 6 x 12 plano-convex lenses, for around $275. The next position would be in the balcony, or, in some instances, in the narthex below where one could highlight a processional down the main aisle. This position calls for a longer throw, possibly a 6 x 22 lens system, and a 750-watt lamp.

With lens specifications, the first figure is the diameter, the second the focal length, and the larger the second figure the narrower the beam and hence the farther the throw.

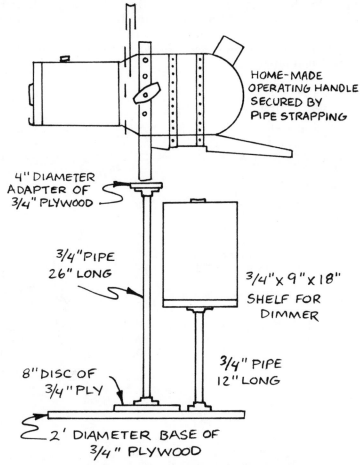

HOME-MADE OPERATING HANDLE SECURED BY PIPE STRAPPING

4" DIAMETER ADAPTER OF 3/4" PLYWOOD

3/4" PIPE 26" LONG

3/4" x 9" x 18" SHELF FOR DIMMER

8" DISC OF 3/4" PLY

3/4" PIPE 12" LONG

2' DIAMETER BASE OF 3/4" PLYWOOD

For many years my favorite was an old eight-inch ellipsoidal into which I inserted an iris control with the help of a welder to cut the necessary slot.

The drawing also indicates the older incandescent lamp whose base must be up (or as nearly so as possible) to avoid lamp meltdown. The new "quartz" lamps are mounted axially, and thus can be inserted into the reflector from center rear, creating a more powerful field of light. However, great care must be taken when fitting these newer lamps into their sockets: no grease or even the natural oil on fingers must touch the quartz bulb, nor are the vacuum seals as rugged as the old incandescents, where a bulb could even fall out of its socket and still be lit!

In studying photometric charts relating to "throws" (the distance the light travels) and brilliance at the subject position, thirty foot-candles is a tolerable level. You are, after all, in a church, and the parishioners are accustomed to as little as five foot-candles in the nave. The chancel may be as bright as fifteen, and special lights for the pulpit and lectern may deliver twenty-five. Also, you are lighting for the human eye, not for film or an orthicon tube behind a camera lens. I once witnessed a very satisfactory performance of Ibsen's *Ghosts* by candlelight at a time when the current had failed.

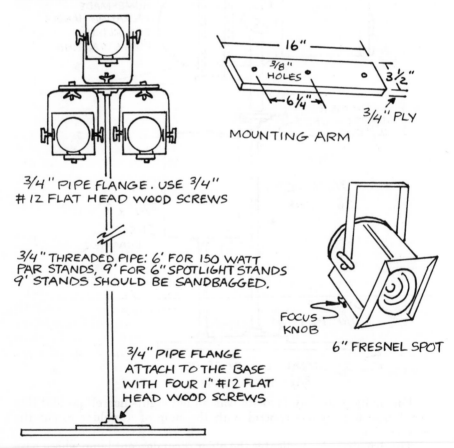

Once dimming needs and an ellipsoidal are in hand, the remaining portable lighting system can be tailored to your budget — you can go homemade all the way or purchase units that are far more economical than ellipsoidal spotlights. The primary lights for church theatricals should be soft-edged, a well-directed "splash" of light which will blend the set pieces and the surrounding church architecture into an aesthetic whole.

The popular six-inch 500-watt Fresnel spotlight produces just such a "splash," a directional soft-edged beam of light whose spread is variable by moving the lamp back and forth within the reflector housing. Here the spotlights are mounted on a homemade stand. The spotlight will include the color frame and a C-clamp suitable for pipe mounting, but not the lamp or electrical connector. You don't need the C-clamp and I'm told it costs more to unpack the box to remove it than the clamp is worth. A six-inch Fresnel spotlight costs about $60 and the lamp about $50.

The next step up in economy is the professional PAR can. PARs are lensless instruments which take rugged sealed beam reflector lamps in a variety of sizes, shapes and wattages. The smallest take the 150- to 300-watt PAR lamps, and these are the ones recommended for our church use. Don't underrate these simple instruments, the PAR 64s, from 500 to 1,000 watts, are the backbone of "rock concert" lighting. The can resembles a Fresnel spotlight without the adjustable lamp base. They do have color frames. The 150- to 300-watt cans cost about $35, the 150-watt lamp, easily available from hardware stores and building supply centers, cost under $10, the 300-watt, not always a local shelf item, is slightly more.

The PAR 38 can take a lamp with a medium screw base. At this point we move into homemade lighting fixtures, for a medium screw base is readily available in many lamp holder devices sold right off the hardware store and building supply center shelves. Cleated sockets are also found in most hardware stores. With these, plus some large vegetable cans, a variety of floodlights can be fashioned that are only limited by your imagination. The down side will be the attachment of color frames of some sort for most of these solutions, for color media (commonly and perhaps erroneously called "gels") must not contact the lamps. They are also flexible enough to require some sort of frame.

Those of you who are familiar with my **Stage Lighting in the Boondocks** will remember an early unit I made up in conjunction with Olesen's #26100 Gelatine Holder and Gel Frame which clips to a PAR lamp. My design includes a large vegetable can to mask the rear of the lamp from audience view. The down side of my fixture is the cleated socket — these are not really designed for this much current and are prone to burning out.

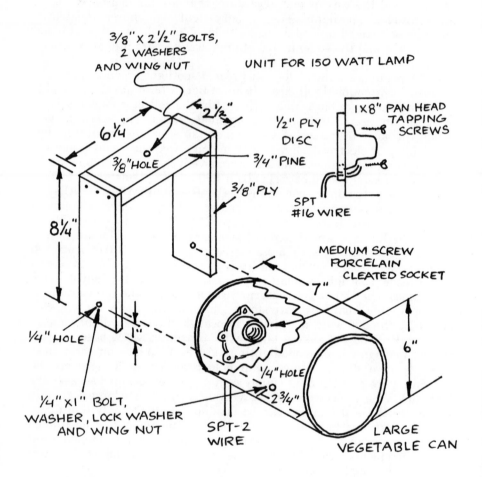

3/8" x 2½" BOLTS,
2 WASHERS
AND WING NUT

UNIT FOR 150 WATT LAMP

6¼"

2½"

½" PLY
DISC

3/8" HOLE

3/4" PINE

3/8" PLY

1X8" PAN HEAD
TAPPING
SCREWS

SPT
#16 WIRE

8¼"

MEDIUM SCREW
PORCELAIN
CLEATED SOCKET

7"

¼" HOLE

1"

¼" HOLE

6"

¼" x 1" BOLT,
WASHER, LOCK WASHER
AND WING NUT

SPT-2
WIRE

2¾"

LARGE
VEGETABLE CAN

68

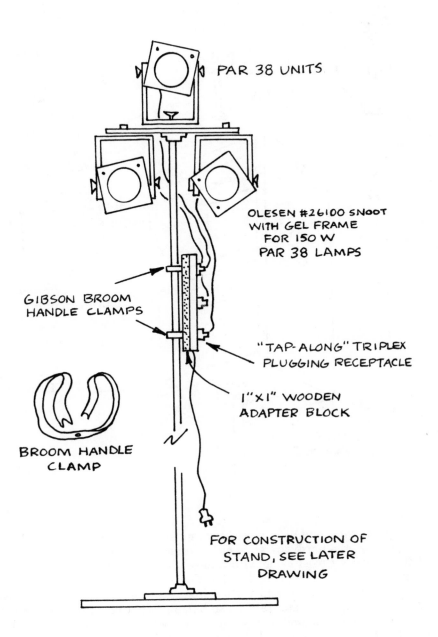

PAR 38 UNITS

OLESEN #26100 SNOOT
WITH GEL FRAME
FOR 150 W
PAR 38 LAMPS

GIBSON BROOM
HANDLE CLAMPS

"TAP-ALONG" TRIPLEX
PLUGGING RECEPTACLE

1" X 1" WOODEN
ADAPTER BLOCK

BROOM HANDLE
CLAMP

FOR CONSTRUCTION OF
STAND, SEE LATER
DRAWING

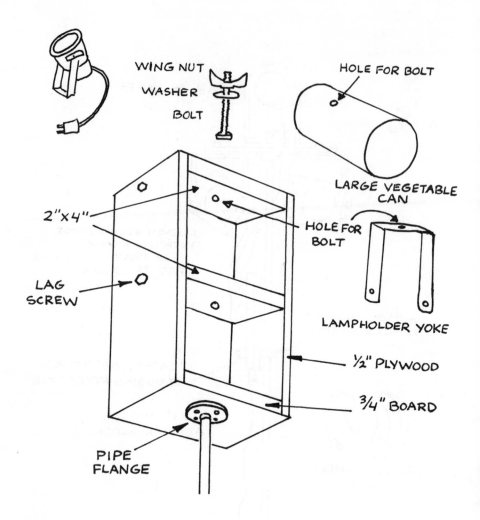

WING NUT

WASHER

BOLT

HOLE FOR BOLT

LARGE VEGETABLE CAN

2"x4"

HOLE FOR BOLT

LAG SCREW

LAMPHOLDER YOKE

½" PLYWOOD

¾" BOARD

PIPE FLANGE

A sturdier and even more economical unit that starts with a lamp-holder from the hardware store or building supply center is shown upper left. The ones I used came with a base plate to fit a standard electrical box plus an L-shaped ground stake. You need only the yoke and socket. Then remove both top and bottom from a large six-inch vegetable can found at a nearby restaurant trash barrel. Slip a bolt through the yoke (you will have to temporarily remove the socket), then up through a hole in the can, then through a hole in the 2 x 4. The 2 x 4 is lag-screwed into the one-half inch plywood sides of the unit so that it can be tilted since you may not have enough play in the yoke for upward or downward adjustment. Bolting some small angle irons to the can will secure a color frame. Spray all parts flat black.

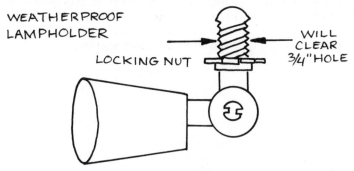

WEATHERPROOF
LAMPHOLDER

LOCKING NUT

WILL
CLEAR
3/4" HOLE

In this ever-changing world, the last time I checked my hardware and building supply stores I could not find the yoked lampholder but found plenty of these security light brackets which screw into dual outlet boxes for placement under the eaves of homes. I was able to purchase the single piece shown for considerably less than the yoked bracket. By notching the 2 x 4 and nailing a piece of 3/8" or 1/4" ply across the notch this bracket can be secured through a 3/4" hole by means of the locking washer.

I like to make up these vertical strip units with three to four lamps, although taller strips may be necessary to build up a sufficient volume of light. This is something we haven't discussed — but the whole subject of brilliance is so relative that adding up foot-candles is unnecessary. A rule of thumb may be useful: if you double the number of lights aimed at a particular target you will get half as much again of that brilliance. Adding a third light will give us a fourth as much again. For example: if your initial reading is twenty foot-candles, aiming a second light will raise the reading to about thirty, and the third light to a total of thirty-five. This is called "the waterfall" principle by illuminating engineers.

Another inexpensive method of mounting lamp receptacles is "track lighting" where adjustable lampholders clamp onto metal sleeves complete with inbuilt circuits. I find these assemblies most useful for floor-based mounting behind ground rows. Track lighting parts are found in home building supply centers along with 50-watt R-40 medium screw base lamps, although a wide variety of other lamps can be used for low level illumination.

I would begin by avoiding color filters entirely. There's not going to be much light to begin with so you really can't afford to lose any through absorption. Also color filters, or "gels," as they are called, are expensive. If you want to try them, I suggest you study my book **Stage Lighting in the Boondocks** before you purchase any. And send for a catalog and a swatch book from Rosco Laboratories, 36 Bush Ave., Port Chester, New York 10573.

Obviously there are going to be quite a few electrical cords strewn about, much of them on the floor. Across aisles, etc. such cables should be taped down as flatly as possible with silver gray duct tape. And since the loads aren't great I use #16 SJ wire (save for the dimmer board connections to the 20-amp wall outlets — which should be #14). It also goes without saying that these cables should be completely removed and stored after each use, not only because it is unwise to leave them unattended but also because you will be gingerly skirting many electrical codes.

A Short Glossary of Perhaps Unfamiliar Terms

Dimmer, *a device by which the intensity of stage illumination can be varied.*

Fresnel, *a spotlight lens which creates a soft-edged field of light, after A. J. Fresnel, an early lighthouse lens designer.*

Gel, *a popular term for a stage lighting color filter, derived from the use of gelatine sheets in which dyes were suspended, a practice largely obsolete.*

Props, *from property, in theatrical usage, furniture and ornaments, or any object handled and used by actors, as distinguished from scenery.*

Velcro, *a synthetic fastening device used in dressmaking, based on the principle of the thistle attaching itself to a passerby.*

Venue, *primarily a legal term meaning place, but now used as the scene of any action or event.*

Serviteur de la scène, *a French term referring to a neutrally costumed actor who assists with set changes while keeping as low a profile as possible.*

Set piece, *a piece of scenery, usually three dimensional, built to stand independently on the stage floor.*

Sonotube, *the building supply trade name for a giant cardboard tube of sufficient strength to contain wet concrete, used for pouring columns and later peeled off.*

About the Author

James Hull Miller, a graduate of Princeton, combines an academic background in literature and philosophy with many years of actual theatre experience of which twelve were spent in teaching. Since 1958 he has been a free lance designer and consultant. His field of special interest is the development of a new stagecraft for the theatre which takes the form of *freestanding scenery*. He has designed numerous open stage theatres based on this system of stagecraft for colleges, communities, student unions, schools and churches. For many years he maintained a scenic studio, the **Arts Lab,** in Shreveport, Louisiana, where he gave workshops as well as constructed sets for use in a variety of spaces. A filmstrip on self-supporting scenery that was photographed in the lab is available from Contemporary Drama Service. Other titles currently available include **Self-Supporting Scenery** (the basic text), **Stage Lighting in the Boondocks,** and **Small Stage Sets on Tour.**

Miller is a Charter Member of the U.S. Institute for Theatre Technology and in 1978 was named a Fellow of the Institute. He is a Founding Member of the American Society of Theatre Consultants. Presently he lives in Charlottesville, Virginia.

ORDER FORM

 MERIWETHER PUBLISHING LTD.
P.O. BOX 7710
COLORADO SPRINGS, CO 80933
TELEPHONE: (719) 594-4422

Please send me the following books:

_____**Stagecraft for Christmas and Easter Plays
#TT-B170**   **$6.95**
by James Hull Miller
A simplified method of staging in the church

_____**Small Stage Sets on Tour #TT-B102**   **$7.95**
by James Hull Miller
A practical guide to portable stage sets

_____**Stage Lighting in the Boondocks #TT-B141**   **$5.95**
by James Hull Miller
A simplified guide to stage lighting

_____**Self-Supporting Scenery #TT-B105**   **$8.95**
by James Hull Miller
A scenic workbook for the open stage

_____**57 Original Auditions for Actors #TT-B181**   **$6.95**
by Eddie Lawrence
A workbook of monologs for actors

_____**Theatre Games for Young Performers #TT-B188** **$7.95**
by Maria C. Novelly
Improvisations and exercises for developing acting skills

_____**Winning Monologs for Young Actors #TT-B127** **$7.95**
by Peg Kehret
Honest-to-life monologs for young actors

> *I understand that I may return any book
> for a full refund if not satisfied.*

NAME: _____

ORGANIZATION NAME: _____

ADDRESS: _____

CITY: _____ STATE:_____ ZIP:_____

PHONE: _____

☐ **Check Enclosed**
☐ **Visa or Master Card #**_____

Signature: _____
(required for Visa/Mastercard orders)

COLORADO RESIDENTS: Please add 3% sales tax.
SHIPPING: Include $1.50 for the first book and 50¢ for each additional book ordered.

☐ *Please send me a copy of your complete catalog of books or plays.*

ORDER FORM

 MERIWETHER PUBLISHING LTD.
P.O. BOX 7710
COLORADO SPRINGS, CO 80933
TELEPHONE: (719) 594-4422

Please send me the following books:

_____**Stagecraft for Christmas and Easter Plays**
#TT-B170 $6.95
by James Hull Miller
A simplified method of staging in the church

_____**Small Stage Sets on Tour #TT-B102** $7.95
by James Hull Miller
A practical guide to portable stage sets

_____**Stage Lighting in the Boondocks #TT-B141** $5.95
by James Hull Miller
A simplified guide to stage lighting

_____**Self-Supporting Scenery #TT-B105** $8.95
by James Hull Miller
A scenic workbook for the open stage

_____**57 Original Auditions for Actors #TT-B181** $6.95
by Eddie Lawrence
A workbook of monologs for actors

_____**Theatre Games for Young Performers #TT-B188** $7.95
by Maria C. Novelly
Improvisations and exercises for developing acting skills

_____**Winning Monologs for Young Actors #TT-B127** $7.95
by Peg Kehret
Honest-to-life monologs for young actors

*I understand that I may return any book
for a full refund if not satisfied.*

NAME: _____

ORGANIZATION NAME: _____

ADDRESS: _____

CITY: _____ STATE:_____ ZIP:_____

PHONE: _____

☐ **Check Enclosed**
☐ **Visa or Master Card #**_____

Signature: _____
(required for Visa/Mastercard orders)

COLORADO RESIDENTS: Please add 3% sales tax.
SHIPPING: Include $1.50 for the first book and 50¢ for each additional book ordered.

☐ *Please send me a copy of your complete catalog of books or plays.*

NOTES

NOTES